# WESLEY R. WILLIS

## VICTOR BOOKS®

A DIVISION OF SCRIPTURE PRESS PUBLICATIONS INC.
USA CANADA ENGLAND

Recommended Dewey Decimal Classification: 227.8
Suggested Subject Heading: BIBLE, N.T.—PAULINE EPISTLES

Library of Congress Catalog Card Number: 88-60204
ISBN: 0-89693-463-2

VICTOR BOOKS
A division of SP Publications, Inc.
        Wheaton, Illinois 60187

# CONTENTS

# How to Use This Study

Personal Growth Bible Studies are designed to help you understand God's Word and how it applies to everyday life. To complete the studies in this book, you will need to use a Bible. A good modern translation of the Bible, such as the *New International Version* or the *New American Standard Bible*, will give you the most help. (NOTE: the questions in this book are based on the *New International Version.*)

You will find it helpful to follow a similar sequence with each study. First, read the introductory paragraphs. This material helps set the tone and lay the groundwork for the passage to be studied. Once you have completed this part of the study, spend time reading the assigned passage in your Bible. This will give you a general feel for the contents of the passage.

Having completed the preliminaries, you are then ready to dig deeper into the Scripture passage. Each study is divided into several sections so that you can take a close-up look at the smaller parts of the larger passage. These sections each begin with a synopsis of the Scripture to be studied in that section. Following each synopsis is a two-part study section made up of *Explaining the Text* and *Examining the Text.*

*Explaining the Text* gives background notes and commentary to help you understand points in the text that may not be readily apparent. After reading any comments that appear in *Explaining the Text,* answer each question under *Examining the Text.*

At the end of each study is a section called *Experiencing the Text.* The questions in this section focus on the application of biblical principles to life. You may find that some of the questions can be answered immediately; others will require that you spend more time reflecting on the passages you have just studied.

The distinctive format of the Personal Growth Bible Studies makes them easy to use individually as well as for group study. If the majority of those in your group answer the questions before the group meeting, spend most of your time together discussing the *Experiencing* questions.

If, on the other hand, members have not answered the questions ahead of time and you have adequate time in your group meeting, work through all of the questions together.

However you use this series of studies, our prayer is that you will understand the Bible as never before, and that because of this understanding, you will experience a rich and dynamic Christian life. If questions of interpretation arise in the course of this study, we recommend you refer to the two-volume set, *The Bible Knowledge Commentary*, edited by John F. Walvoord and Roy B. Zuck (Victor Books, 1984, 1986).

# Introduction to the Epistle to the Philippians

Sometimes it seems that every time I turn around another person is suggesting a surefire strategy for success. But many of these define success very strangely. Books are written and published that ostensibly tell us how to live. Newspapers report stories about those who made it big. Magazines run feature articles that tell us how to succeed. Celebrities are interviewed on television and recount their secrets of success.

And yet many of these champions of "successful living" promote ideas that are contradictory, if not outright stupid. One man "succeeds" because he began buying savings bonds at age six. Another hit it big in the lottery. One person is into meditation and Eastern religion, while another advocates a libertarian view of life. One person finds success in sports, another in the arts, and still a third in "living off the land." Who is to say which is the true way to a full and meaningful life?

In his letter to the Philippians, the Apostle Paul explained God's idea of a successful life. The Philippians had made a good start in the Christian life, but they needed help and encouragement. And so Paul, living under house arrest in Rome, wrote to explain God's secret.

The letter to the Philippians describes six principles which explain how to live a full and meaningful life. And to be sure that no one would miss the message, Paul followed each principle with illustrations of people who applied that principle in their lives. However, achieving success in each of these areas is not automatic and does not come without problems. And so we find that we need to deal with difficulties too.

Philippians also addresses those problems that will keep us from experiencing a full life. I pray that as you study this book, you will avoid the problems and you will experience the full life in Christ that He intended for you

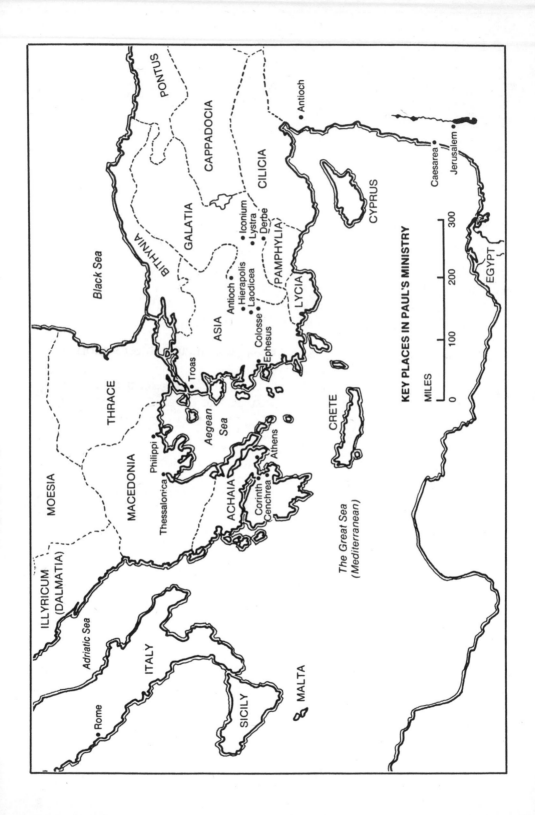

KEY PLACES IN PAUL'S MINISTRY

# Philippians 1:1-26

## Developing Spiritual Discernment

Anyone who has tried to live on a limited budget is keenly aware of the need for discernment. Take grocery shopping for instance; sometimes it seems as though manufacturers go out of their way to try to confuse shoppers. When the per-ounce price of the "large economy size" exceeds the per-ounce price of the "regular size," the manufacturer's motivation clearly should be called into question.

Have you tried to buy a car lately? Now that's an exercise in discernment! After observing the advertisements, and carefully studying all of the literature available, you go out and begin to shop. You travel from one showroom to another examining the different makes and models and finally you are ready to make a purchase. At first you try to order a basic model with several accessories. But no, you can't order it that way. Those accessories only come in packages. Of course the packages include many features that you don't want. "But," the salesman cheerfully informs you, "for less than the price of any accessory package, you can order a deluxe model." Of course that model includes even more items you don't need, and it costs several thousand dollars more. When it comes to buying automobiles, we all need discernment!

Just as we need discernment in purchasing decisions, we also need discernment in spiritual decisions. Some things are good, but other things are better. And in order to reach full maturity in Christ we must become spiritually discerning—able to evaluate and conclude what is best. Paul prayed that the Philippians would develop the ability to discern the Spirit's leading in their own lives—to distinguish between what is merely good and what is God's best.

A. INTRODUCTION AND PURPOSE OF PHILIPPIANS (*Phil. 1:1-8*). Today, we write our names at the conclusion of our letters. But in Paul's day, an author began by identifying both himself and the recipient. Following his normal opening (which included wishing the Philippians both grace and peace), Paul stated his purpose for writing—that the Philippians would come to *full maturity* in Christ.

---

*Examining the Text*

1. Read Philippians 1:1-8. How does Paul describe himself and Timothy? Bond servants of Jesus Christ.

What does this suggest to you about Paul's attitude toward the Philippians and his relationship with them?

2. What three groups of people were the recipients of this letter? (v. 1)

Saints
Overseers (Bishops)
Deacons

3. What two qualities did Paul desire for the Philippians? (v. 2) Grace and peace

What was the source of these qualities?

God the Father
Lord Jesus Christ

4. How would you describe Paul's feelings toward the Philippian believers? (vv. 3-4, 7-8)

Thankful for them - lifting them up in prayer.
Longs for them with affection of Christ.

*Explaining the Text*

1. Since he was well known by the Philippians, Paul probably felt it wasn't necessary to identify himself as an apostle.

2. A bishop (*episkopos*) was an overseer. The word often is used with "elder" to indicate a shepherding function (Acts 20:17, 20; Titus 1:5, 7; 1 Peter 5:1-2).

3. This is a typical benediction which Paul used frequently at the beginning of his letters. Sometimes "mercy" is also included.

*Explaining the Text*

5. The Philippian's partnership (*koinonia*) probably included the sharing of personal and community resources, time, friendship, emotional and financial support, and prayer.

6. Verse 6 could be taken as the key verse for the entire letter. It is essentially a summary of the normal Christian life.

*Examining the Text*

5. Why did he rejoice on behalf of the Philippians? (v. 5)

*Because of their participating in the gospel from the beginning until now.*

6. What did Paul expect that God would do in the Philippians' lives? (v. 6)

*Confident that He who began a good work will perfect it until the day of Jesus Christ.*

7. Think about your own church community. How have you seen God working, completing the good work He began in you?

---

B. THE QUALITY OF SPIRITUAL DISCERNMENT (*Phil. 1:9-11*). This passage presents the first of Paul's principles for successfully living the Christian life. This principle relates to spiritual discernment. We must recognize those things that are excellent and that glorify God.

---

*Explaining the Text*

2. Spiritual discernment involves the cognitive (mental) and the the moral dimensions of life. Morality naturally follows (and is guided by) true spiritual knowledge (understanding).

*Examining the Text*

1. Read Philippians 1:9-11. What was Paul's prayer for the Philippian believers? (v. 9)

*Love may abound still more and more in real knowledge and all discernment.*

2. What should be the moral quality of those who are truly discerning? (v. 10)

*Approve the things that are excellent. In order to be sincere blameless until the day of Christ.*

| Examining the Text | Explaining the Text |
|---|---|
| 3. What will characterize the life of a person who practices discernment in both its moral and cognitive dimensions? (v. 11) | 3. Our moral values affect how we respond to life's circumstances. |

*Being filled with the fruit of righteousness*

4. In what areas of your day-to-day life do you feel the need for more (or better) discernment?

*Talking with others. Reactions to circumstances*

## C. PAUL'S EXAMPLE OF SPIRITUAL DISCERNMENT (*Phil. 1:12-18*).

You've probably heard the expression "Talk is cheap." But in Paul's life, it was not mere talk when he challenged believers to spiritual discernment. He himself had been arrested and suffered great persecution. And yet Paul praised God because he realized that his difficult circumstances had contributed to the spread of the Gospel.

| Examining the Text | Explaining the Text |
|---|---|
| 1. Read Philippians 1:12-18. What were Paul's circumstances at the time of the writing of this letter? (v. 13) | |
| *Imprisonment* | |
| 2. What was one benefit of Paul's negative circumstances? (v. 12) | 2. "The whole palace guard" refers both to those assigned to guard Paul (who was under house arrest) and also to the other soldiers who served with those guards. |

*Turned out for the greater progress of the Gospel*

| Explaining the Text | Examining the Text |
|---|---|
| 3. "Brothers in the Lord" (v. 14) refers to fellow Christians—persons who had accepted salvation by faith in Christ. | 3. How were other Christians influenced by Paul's circumstances? (v. 14) *They had more courage to speak the Word of God without fear.* |
| | 4. What were the two reasons for which people were preaching the Gospel of Christ? (vv. 15-17) *Envy & strife — some from good. out of love Selfish ambitions* |
| 5. Apparently, even though the motivation of some preachers was incorrect, God still derived honor from the proclamation. | 5. How does Paul's response demonstrate an uncommon level of true spiritual discernment? (v. 18) *Christ is proclaimed! whether in pretense or in TRUTH* |

**D. THE RESULTS OF SPIRITUAL DISCERNMENT** (*Phil. 1:19-26*). Paul's faith in the goodness of God enabled him to live a life marked by joy and peace. He was not blind to problems, but his spiritual discernment enabled him to see beyond them.

| Explaining the Text | Examining the Text |
|---|---|
| 1. Comfort and convenience seem to have been far less important to Paul than the spiritual goals that guided and motivated his life. | 1. Read Philippians 1:19-26. Restate in your own words Paul's summary of his spiritually determined life goals (vv. 20-21). *Paul would not be put to shame but would preach with all boldness. Christ will always be exalted in his body. Whether by life or death* |
| | 2. What two possibilities did Paul envision as potential outcomes of his imprisonment? (vv. 22-23) *1. To live on — more fruitful labor. 2. Desire to depart to be with Christ which is better. To remain in the flesh for their sakes.* |

*Examining the Text*

3. Which of the two possibilities did Paul seem to prefer emotionally? Which of the two did he expect to actually occur? (vv. 23-26)

*Hard pressed in both direction yet was convinced he would remain here.*

*Explaining the Text*

3. True spiritual discernment includes a perspective that values the welfare of others, as well as our own personal benefits.

---

*Experiencing the Text*

1. In what ways could we serve as partners in the Gospel even as the Philippian believers did? *To proclaim Christ*

Choose one way in which you will put "partnership" into practice this week. What do you need to carry out this plan?

2. In what areas of your life do you feel that God is presently working to bring you to fuller maturity?

3. What difficulties have you been (or might you be) called to experience as you seek to serve God?

4. Write out a prayer, asking God to help you develop discernment in your life.

# Philippians 1:27–2:11

## Serving with Spiritual Strength

One of the continuing popular themes in contemporary culture is the theme of the independent, self-sufficient loner. One version of this theme is the macho man who is tough and strong and doesn't need anyone. At the end of the drama he rides off into the sunset with people standing in awe of his strength and independence.

The independent woman has become a popular theme too. She is elegant in bearing, regal in her demeanor. When she wafts into the room, a hush falls over the crowd—they stand in awe. Her taste is impeccable, her clothing immaculate. People await her beck and call. And when she is finished with them, she discards them as easily as most of us toss out yesterday's newspaper.

What is being sold in all of these scenarios is an outright, blatant lie. It is a lie that says the independent life is the desirable life. It is a lie that says the ideal person is the one who doesn't have to depend on anyone else, and who is free from responsibility. It is a lie that says we will be happier when we direct our own lives, and don't need to worry about anyone else.

Paul clearly taught the Philippians that in order to experience life as God intended, we need to stand strong for the Gospel. But we can't do this alone. Each of us needs to look for ways to provide support and encouragement to others—ways to minister to them. Paul illustrated this from the life of Jesus Christ who had the rights and privileges that many desire. And yet He relinquished them. Jesus humbled Himself and sacrificed those rights. He is our example.

A. THE QUALITY OF SPIRITUAL STRENGTH (*Phil. 1:27-28*). Most of us have no idea what we would do if suddenly we were thrust into a life-or-death situation. If such a situation arose, we hope that we would be strong and resolute. However, most of us never will have to face such a problem. But daily we are confronted with spiritual conflicts. And in these we also need strength to stand, strong and unflinching.

| *Examining the Text* | *Explaining the Text* |
|---|---|
| 1. Read Philippians 1:27-28. What manner of life did Paul expect from the Philippians? (v. 27) | |
| 2. In what ways might these qualities be demonstrated today by a person leading a life worthy of the Gospel? (v. 27) | 2. The last part of verse 27 describes the qualities of a person who is leading a life worthy of the Gospel. |
| 3. For what did Paul expect the Philippians to contend? (v. 27)<br><br>And against whom were they to contend? (v. 28) | |
| 4. What ought to be the attitude of believers as they contend for the faith of the Gospel? (v. 27) | 4. Notice that contentiousness was not supposed to be the attitude among believers. Rather, the contending should be against those who are opposed to the Gospel. |
| 5. How should believers relate to those who may be opposed to the Gospel? (v. 28) | |

| *Explaining the Text* | *Examining the Text* |
|---|---|
| 6. Apparently the "sign" is an indicator that grows out of the fact that there is unity and stability (even in tribulation) among believers. | 6. What is the different impact of the "sign" on believers and unbelievers as they observe it? (v. 28) |

**B. THE NEED FOR STRENGTH** (*Phil. 1:29-30*). At some time or other in life, most of us will warn someone else about what that person will face. Parents tell children, and supervisors tell new employees. But many times the warning is ignored. In this section, Paul explains what believers can expect.

| *Explaining the Text* | *Examining the Text* |
|---|---|
| | 1. Read Philippians 1:29-30. What can believers in Jesus Christ expect to experience as they seek to live for Him? (v. 29) |
| 2. "The same struggle" probably referred to the persecution that Philippian believers were experiencing due to their faith in Jesus Christ. | 2. Who experienced the same sort of personal struggle that the Philippians were going through? (v. 30) |
| 3. Compare similar teachings in James 1:2-4; 1 Peter 1:1-7; 4:12-14. | 3. How should we respond to those who claim that by accepting Christ we no longer will suffer problems or pain? |

**C. MINISTERING FROM STRENGTH** (*Phil. 2:1-4*). All of us understand that when certain conditions exist, we do certain things. "Because it is raining today, I will take my umbrella." According to God's Word, certain conditions exist for believers. And because they do, we should act in appropriate ways.

| *Examining the Text* | *Explaining the Text* |
|---|---|
| 1. Read Philippians 2:1-4. List below the four conditions that exist for those united with Christ that enable them to support, strengthen, and encourage one another (v. 1). | 1. The four "if" phrases in verse 1 indicate a certain contingency. This particular construction is one of four ways to say "if" in Greek. In this case the argument rests on the reality of the conditions. Therefore, it is appropriate to translate each "if" with the word "since." |

*Since . . .*

*Since . . .*

*Since . . .*

*Since . . .*

| | |
|---|---|
| 2. Paul indicated that his joy would be complete when the Philippians were united in four areas. What are these four areas? (v. 2) | 2. Spiritual unity does not mean that we all think the same things, dress alike, share the same political beliefs, or practice the same daily rituals. It does mean that we have certain basic beliefs and attitudes in common. These are the basis of unity. |

3. Paraphrase Paul's admonition on how we should not act as believers.

| | |
|---|---|
| 4. What is the proper motivation that should guide believers? (vv. 3-4) | 4. Paul's point in verse 3 is *not* that believers should ignore their own needs and interests, but that our individual interests should not be our total pre-occupation. Rather than only looking out for "number one," we also bear responsibility for each other. |

| Explaining the Text | Examining the Text |
|---|---|
| | Paraphrase Paul's instruction on the proper motivation to guide in relationships |

D. CHRIST'S EXAMPLE OF MINISTERING FROM STRENGTH (*Phil. 2:5-11*). Most of us have trouble understanding abstract ideas. So in order to help us grasp what it means to be strong and to minister to others in that strength, Paul gives us a concrete example of how we ought to serve  He challenged us to serve as Christ served

| Explaining the Text | Examining the Text |
|---|---|
| 1. Jesus, the Son of God, deserved all of the privileges due Him as God. And yet He did not demand those rights ("something to be grasped"). Instead He voluntarily relinquished them. | 1. Read Philippians 2:5-11. Jesus Christ is the prime example of humble service. His selfless attitude can be seen by His willingness to relinquish His rights in order to serve others. What was He willing to give up? (v. 6) |
| 2. The key element in each step that Jesus took was His humility ("made Himself nothing" v. 7, "humbled Himself" v. 8). Jesus placed the welfare of others above His personal preferences, even above the rightful exercise of His position in the Godhead. | 2. In relinquishing the rights of Deity, Jesus made several steps down—all the way to the cross. What was each step, and what do you think each step meant for Jesus?<br><br>*Step 1* (v. 7)<br><br>*Step 2* (v. 7)<br><br>*Step 3* (v. 8)<br><br>*Step 4* (v 8) |
| 3. There is a basic spiritual principle demonstrated in this passage. When obedience to God puts us in a difficult position, God | 3. What two things did God choose to do for Jesus since Jesus willingly humbled Himself? (v. 9) |

*Examining the Text*

*Explaining the Text*

Himself intervenes on
our behalf and provides for
our spiritual needs.

4. What will be the ultimate result of what God will
do in glorifying Jesus? (vv. 10-11)

*Experiencing the Text*

1. What do you need in order to be able to "stand firm in one spirit"?

2. What struggles might we experience as we stand up for the spiritual principles
that we claim to believe?

3. What step will you take in the next week to encourage spiritual unity in your
church?

4. Think through your relationships in the four areas listed below. In each area,
what would it mean for you to follow the example of Jesus ("He humbled Himself
and became obedient to death")?

Personal life?

Family life?

Vocational life?

Ministries?

# Philippians 2:12-30

## Obeying without Complaining

One of my favorite recreational activities is backpacking. With all the gear and food I need in my backpack, I am able to hike from campsite to campsite, enjoying the freedom of mobility and the beauty of the wilderness. Because I am self-contained, remote and otherwise inaccessible areas become available for enjoyment.

Of course one limitation of backpacking is that the camper must carry everything in a pack on his back. This means that great care must be taken in selecting the type and the amount of equipment taken. Obviously, every additional ounce, multiplied by the number of steps taken, demands great exertion. So avid backpackers go to great extremes to limit the weight that they have to carry.

Serious backpackers strive to reduce weight in every imaginable way. They search for multiuse utensils, or look for ways to alter utensils to further lighten the load. For instance, backpackers often cut off part of a utensil handle in order to reduce weight. (A peek into my pack would reveal a "shortie" toothbrush handle.) And in the pack itself, nylon and aluminum are essential materials for minimizing weight.

On one particular backpacking trip with one of my sons, we were camped in a clearing of about one acre. As the night grew darker, we fired up my lantern. No, it wasn't a high-intensity gas lantern. Designed for carrying long distances, it was one candlepower—literally. A tiny aluminum and glass lantern held one slow-burning candle.

When we first lit that candle, it seemed to provide very little light. But as the night grew darker, it shone more and more brightly. By the time we were ready to crawl into our sleeping bags, the tiny flame was casting flickering shadows all the way across the clearing. The small volume of light seemed great because the night was very dark.

As Christians, we provide light for a dark world. And the darker our world becomes, the more brightly we are able to shine.

A. THE IMPORTANCE OF OBEDIENCE (*Phil. 2:12-13*). All of us know people who act one way when they are being watched and another when they are alone. This is never appropriate for the believer. We should practice our Christianity whether anyone is watching or not.

| *Examining the Text* | *Explaining the Text* |
|---|---|
| 1. Read Philippians 2:12-13. How did Paul expect the Philippians to act? (v. 12) | 1. "Dear friends" is a warm, personal greeting that demonstrates Paul's deep feelings for those to whom he was writing. The Philippians were more than just another group of people making demands on Paul's time. |
| Under what circumstances did Paul expect this mode of behavior? (v. 12) | |
| 2. What does Paul seem to think about the Philippians' behavior previous to his letter? What in verse 12 supports your conclusion? | 2. The phrase "work out your salvation" means "put your faith into practice," or "live out your faith." It does not mean "work to earn your salvation." After a person has accepted salvation by faith, good works are the outgrowth of new life. |
| 3. What is the proper attitude for a believer seeking to live a godly life? (v. 12) | 3. "With fear and trembling" certainly implies that we should *not* have an attitude of self-sufficiency or complacency. We have serious obligations as we live for Christ. |
| 4. What is the key resource that enables us to obey—to live the Christian life consistently? (v. 13) | |

B. THE RESULT OF OBEDIENCE—PLEASANT COMMUNICATION (*Phil. 2:14-18*). Constant griping, complaining, and arguing can be heard in many family and work situations. Of course, we all get frustrated and annoyed from time to time; but the life of a believer should *not* be characterized by complaining and arguing.

| *Explaining the Text* | *Examining the Text* |
|---|---|
| 1. "Complaining" means grumbling or griping, whereas "arguing" suggests more open confrontation or verbal disputing. | 1. Read Philippians 2:14-18. How should we act if we are practicing truly biblical Christianity—living as God intends? (v. 14) |
| 2. "Crooked and depraved generation" refers to those who are not believers—those who reject God's principles as guidance for their lives. | 2. How will people who don't complain and argue be seen by those who are not believers? (v. 15) |
| | 3. Stars are seen best during the darkest part of the night. How does this relate to the way that we live our lives as Christians? (v. 15) |
| 4. To "hold out the word of life" is a concept similar to holding out a life preserver. It means to offer something to another person. Both a life preserver and God's Word offer life—one physical, the other spiritual. | 4. What should be our key goal as we seek to live as God intends? (v. 16) |
| | 5. How did Paul demonstrate the attitude of doing everything without complaining or arguing? (vv. 17-18) |

C. EXAMPLES OF PLEASANT OBEDIENCE (*Phil. 2:19-30*). Examples are usually helpful in understanding a new idea or concept. But they're not always easy to find. For instance, you may know a biblical principle, and you may be able to explain it to others. But until you see how that principle works in real life, you will not fully understand it. Unfortunately, it can be quite difficult locating a visible example—someone actually living-out that principle. Paul was able to cite two Christians who served God and who did it without complaining or arguing.

| *Examining the Text* | *Explaining the Text* |
|---|---|
| 1. Read Philippians 2:19-30. How was Timothy different from others in his attitude toward service? (vv. 19-20) | 1. Timothy was a young man whom Paul had taught and encouraged. He also had traveled with Paul and learned both by verbal instruction and by Paul's example. |
| 2. What was the attitude of most of those whom Paul expected would be serving selflessly? (v. 21) | |
| 3. What does Paul's letter to the Philippians indicate about Timothy's attitude toward Paul? (v. 22) | |
| 4. How was Epaphroditus an example of ungrudging obedience? (vv. 25-27, 30) | 4. Epaphroditus had been sent by the Philippians to deliver gifts to Paul. After arriving, Epaphroditus saw Paul's great need and stayed to help, working very hard in the process. |
| 5. In what ways and to what extent did Paul value the service of Epaphroditus? (vv. 25, 27, 29-30) | 5. Apparently Epaphroditus became ill and almost died while serving Paul. Most likely this was due to neglecting his own needs while ministering to Paul's. |

*Experiencing the Text*

1. What attitude should a Christian have toward obedience?

2. How can we be strengthened to obey God, even when we don't feel like doing those things that we know we should?

3. Describe some people you know who have a willingness to serve as Timothy and Epaphroditus did.

4. Describe some specific steps that you are willing to take to cultivate such an attitude in your own life.

# Philippians 3:1-14

## Cultivating Spiritual Values

All of us change as we grow older. Things that once were terribly important to us now appear to be insignificant. Activities that once consumed great amounts of time have been replaced with other activities.

Recently I was talking to a good friend. I knew that he had been quite an adept trombone player when he was younger. He even had won a competition, giving him the opportunity to play with the U.S. Navy Band. Recently I asked him how long it had been since he played his trombone. He replied, "I haven't touched my horn in over twenty years."

My friend had spent many hours playing in bands and orchestras, and countless hours practicing. Yet that was another part of his life. When I asked why he never played anymore, he explained that he had many other things to do. Playing the trombone was no longer important to him.

When one of our sons was young, he collected milk bottle caps. We never could figure out what the great attraction was. Each cap was identical to every other one. And yet he collected and carefully stored all of the caps that he could get his hands on. When we mentioned it to him recently, he was amazed that he ever did such a thing. He doesn't even remember collecting them. Though his "collection" was important at the time, when he grew older he forgot about it. Now it seems to him to be a silly thing to have done. (We always thought so.)

There is a similar spiritual principle. At one stage in our lives, certain activities, practices, and values are important to us. But as we grow up spiritually, our values change. And those things that once were important fade into insignificance. When the Apostle Paul became a follower of Jesus Christ, he abandoned spiritually useless values; and he challenged the Philippians to follow his example. We too must turn our backs on those things that do not help us to cultivate true spiritual values.

A. CHARACTERISTICS OF SPIRITUAL VALUES (*Phil. 3:1-4a*). Someone once said that a cynic is a person who knows the cost of everything, but the value of nothing. Paul explained to the Philippians that in order to experience full Christianity, we must cultivate a proper value system.

*Examining the Text*

*Explaining the Text*

1. Read Philippians 3:1-4. What ought to be the object of a Christian's rejoicing? (v. 1)

1. It is common among Bible students to emphasize the word "rejoice," but this probably is not the key word. The important element is the *object* of our rejoicing.

2. Even as first-century Jews rejoiced in the Mosaic Law, some people today rejoice in the wrong things. What are some wrong things in which people rejoice?

2. Note the contrast between verses 1 and 2. Some gloried in fleshly (physical) identification (v. 2). Paul gloried in the spiritual value (v. 3). The "dogs" probably refers to Jewish leaders who wrongly claimed that circumcision (fleshly identification) was necessary for salvation (Acts 15:5; cp. 15:8-11).

   In contrast to those earthly values, what *spiritual* things can be our basis for rejoicing?

3. Why do you think Paul spoke with such authority about rejoicing on the basis of fleshly confidence? (v. 4)

B. IMPORTANCE OF REJECTING WRONG VALUES (*Phil. 3:4b-11*). If a person wanted to pass counterfeit money, the worst place to go to would be a bank. Bank tellers handle so much money that they would probably spot and reject a counterfeit bill immediately. When we consider spiritual values, rejecting all false values is just as important as cultivating the proper values.

| *Explaining the Text* | *Examining the Text* |
|---|---|
| 1. Paul presented himself as an example of one who had all of the physical reasons for glorying in the flesh. But these became insignificant when he found that spiritual values were what really counted. | 1. Read Philippians 3:4b-11. Make a list of all the physical reasons why Paul had rejoiced and previously felt confident (vv. 4b-6). |
| | 2. Instead of rejoicing, what attitude did Paul adopt toward these physical values? (v. 7) |
| 3. "Rubbish" (sometimes translated "dung") can mean anything considered worthless, and thrown out. The "all things" that Paul lost were the physical values that could not bring him to Christ or to spiritual maturity. | 3. What did Paul choose to replace those physical values that he had esteemed so highly? (v. 8) |
| | 4. What are the consequences of knowing (having a personal relationship with) Christ? (v. 9) |
| 5. While Paul first described giving up physical values as loss, he then clarified that it was an exchange. He exchanged rubbish for that which has infinite value. | 5. By what means can we have Christ's righteousness counted as our own personal righteousness? (v. 9) |
| | 6. What other benefits did Paul identify that he received by accepting Christ and His righteousness? (v. 10) |

| Examining the Text | Explaining the Text |
|---|---|
| 7. What will be the ultimate benefit of the new relationship that comes through faith in Christ? (v. 11) | 7. "Somehow" does not indicate that there was a question in Paul's mind about whether or not he really would attain. Rather, it means "in some way" or "in any way." |

C. THE PROCESS OF SPIRITUAL GROWTH (*Phil. 3:12-14*). Even though Paul used himself as an example, he was not presumptuous in his position. He knew that he also was in the process of maturing, even as those to whom he was writing, and even as we are today.

| Examining the Text | Explaining the Text |
|---|---|
| 1. What did Paul recognize that he had not gained in his spiritual pilgrimage? (v. 12) | |
| 2. What was Paul's attitude toward his state of maturity when he was writing? (v. 12) | 2. While the last half of verse 12 appears to be confusing ("take hold of that for which Christ took hold of me"), verses 13-14 go on to explain the process that Paul was trying to describe. |
| And what was he doing as a follower of Christ? | |
| 3. What goal had Paul chosen as an alternative to those he had left behind? (vv. 13-14) | 3. What Paul had left behind were the useless, physical things (rubbish) that he had once valued so highly—things that could never bring him to God. |

| Explaining the Text | Examining the Text |
| --- | --- |
|  | 4. What was Paul's attitude as he worked toward his goal of completion (or full maturity) in Jesus Christ? (vv. 13-14) |

## Experiencing the Text

1. What things might you be tempted to value that are rubbish when compared with the reality of knowing Christ and receiving all that He has to offer?

What steps can you take to assure that you will not become preoccupied with impressive earthly/physical values?

2. Have you personally accepted the gift of salvation based on Christ's righteousness? If you haven't, pray a prayer of acceptance right now, thanking God for this gift.

If you have accepted Christ's gift (now, or some time in the past), write a brief prayer to God, expressing how you feel about being a follower of Christ.

3. Since the Apostle Paul recognized that he had not yet arrived, how should we view ourselves?

4. What steps will you take to help cultivate the kind of attitude toward spiritual growth that Paul had?

STUDY FIVE

# Philippians 3:15–4:7

## Living Christianly Every Day

Recently I came across a humorous saying that I had read several years ago.

Those who can, do.

Those who can't do, teach.

And those who can't teach, teach others to teach.

But this time, there was another sentence added to the saying:

And those who can't teach others to teach, write books about it!

Now that hit just a little bit too close to home, since not only have I taught others to teach, but I have also written a book about effective teaching (*Make Your Teaching Count!* Victor, 1985).

Naturally I paused to evaluate the intent behind the quip that I had just read. Did the author really mean to imply that it takes less skill to teach other to do something than it takes to perform the task yourself? And writing books about effective teaching requires the least skill of all? Probably not—I suspect that he was intending to communicate that we need more than just theory; we must be able to practice as well as to preach.

Jesus probably had a similar idea in mind when He explained to His disciples that whatever a teacher *is*, his students will become (Luke 6:40). We teach by example, guiding and directing our students. And in this section of Philippians, Paul stressed the importance of example. He and others set the example for the Philippians (and us) to follow.

A. QUALITY OF CHRISTIAN LIVING (*Phil. 3:15-16*). Have you ever heard someone tell another person to act his age? Usually this is an insult, implying that the person is acting in a childish manner. Paul instructed the Philippians to act their *spiritual* age—to live Christianly.

| Examining the Text | Explaining the Text |
|---|---|
| 1. Read Philippians 3:15-16. What should be the perspective from which we view life? (v. 15) | 1. "Such a view" probably refers back to verse 14, where Paul expressed his desire to "press on toward the goal." |
| 2. Who will be the source of the new, different perspective if presently we have the wrong view of life? (v. 15) | 2. Apparently Paul was convinced that any Christians who really were in the process of maturing would have their incorrect impressions corrected. |
| 3. By what standard should we measure ourselves? (v. 16) | 3. Because there are many variables that influence growth and maturity, all Christians will not develop at the same rate. |
| 4. Knowing that we each mature spiritually at our own rate, how do you feel about the pressure of comparing yourself with other Christians and their expectations for you? | |

B. PAUL'S EXAMPLE OF LIVING CHRISTIANLY (*Phil. 3:17–4:1*). Just as a picture is worth a thousand words, so is a good example. In this case, Paul offered himself as a positive example, and then contrasted this with the negative example of the enemies of the Cross.

*Explaining the Text*

1. Paul was not encouraging people to follow him as a person, but as an example of one following Christ (v. 14).

2. Apparently Paul felt so deeply about what he was writing that it even caused him to weep over the situation.

4. Citizenship describes the ultimate object of our allegiance, and the source of our values and beliefs. Though we live in another culture for a period of time, our values and beliefs should not change. We remain citizens of our mother country.

5. Even though we are citizens of heaven, we experience all of the physical limitations and the resulting difficulties for as long as we live here on earth.

*Examining the Text*

1. Read Philippians 3:17–4:1. What was the pattern of maturity that believers were to follow? (v. 17)

2. What was the cause of Paul's great grief? (v. 18)

3. How did Paul describe those who were not living according to the pattern that he had given the Philippians? (vv. 18-19)

4. Even though we are presently living on earth, we are actually citizens of heaven. When will we experience all of the benefits of this heavenly citizenship? (vv. 20-21)

5. What benefits did Paul describe that believers in Christ ultimately will receive? (vv. 20-21)

6. How should the fact that we are citizens of heaven, and not of this world, affect the way that we confront daily problems and opportunities?

C. THE EXAMPLES OF EUODIA AND SYNTYCHE (*Phil. 4:2-3*). Even though believers have heavenly citizenship, sometimes our behavior is more like the citizens of this world. Euodia and Syntyche were two such persons.

| Examining the Text | Explaining the Text |
|---|---|
| 1. Read Philippians 4:2-3. What change of behavior did Paul want to take place in the lives of Euodia and Syntyche? (v. 2) | 1. Euodia, which means "prosperous journey," and Syntyche, which means "pleasant acquaintance," apparently were not living up to their names. |
| 2. What was the basis on which these two women should have agreed with each other? (v. 3) | |
| 3. How had Euodia and Syntyche worked with Paul in the past? (v. 3) | 3. There were many believers in Philippi who had worked with Paul at various times. |

D. PRINCIPLES FOR LIVING CHRISTIANLY (*Phil. 4:4-7*). The Christian life is far more than a list of do's and don'ts. However, there *are* guidelines for living. Paul concluded this section by summarizing some of these guidelines.

| Examining the Text | Explaining the Text |
|---|---|
| 1. Read Philippians 4:4-7. How should we respond to any (and every) situation in which we find ourselves? (v. 4) | |
| What does this mean to you in your daily responsibilities? | |

*Explaining the Text*

2. We should have a gentle spirit as we respond to each other.

*Examining the Text*

2. Why should gentleness be characteristic of the Christian life? (v. 5)

3. What alternative to anxiety (worry) did Paul suggest? (v. 6)

4. Praying to God about those things that concern us will bring a settled state that is incomprehensible (passes all understanding).

4. What will be the ultimate result of going to God with our petitions and prayers? (v. 7)

*Experiencing the Text*

1. As you have matured in your Christian life, in what attitudes and/or actions have you seen change?

What brought about these changes?

2. In what way does dissension among believers hinder the progress of the Gospel?

What are some ways in which we can prevent such hindrance from occurring?

3. What suggestions would you give to a person seeking to develop a gentle spirit and a worry-free life?

4. Is your life characterized by gentleness and lack of worry? Why or why not?

What would it mean for you if gentleness were more characteristic of your life?

# Philippians 4:8-23

## Thinking Spiritual Thoughts

We have accepted a great divorce in today's society. And because of this divorce, we are paying the penalty in more ways and at a far greater price than we could ever imagine. I'm referring to the divorce of thoughts from behavior. We compartmentalize life, cutting it into neat little segments, believing that we can keep the segments totally separate from each other.

We're probably all guilty of this. We dismiss the idea that watching violence on television will affect our behavior. We watch shows that depict (or imply) adultery, sexual perversion, materialism, and countless other anti-Christian views of life. We read books and magazines that are, at best, mindless; and then are surprised when we find it difficult to concentrate on spiritual matters. We are amazed to find ourselves doing things that we never imagined possible. But we shouldn't be surprised. If we sow the seeds of inappropriate behavior in our thought lives, we should not be surprised when they bear fruit.

Our thought lives have a powerful impact on our behavior. If we are preoccupied with and concentrate on ungodly topics, we will act in un-Christian ways. Paul's final plea to the Philippians was to guard their thoughts so that they could experience full Christian lives.

A. APPROPRIATE SPIRITUAL THOUGHTS (*Phil. 4:8-9*). The Book of Proverbs says that a person becomes what he thinks about. "Above all else, guard your heart, for it is the wellspring of life" (Prov. 4:23). But many people are sloppy in their thought lives, and so they do not experience the joy and fullness of the Christian life.

| *Examining the Text* | *Explaining the Text* |
|---|---|
| 1. List below the appropriate thoughts described in verse 8. Then select a word to describe the opposite of each of these thoughts. | 1. The word "finally" (v. 8) indicates the end of the series of topics written to help believers experience full and complete Christian lives. In verse 8, Paul described six characteristics of a healthy thought life. Each characteristic is introduced by the word "whatever." "Think on" means "to concentrate" or "weigh in one's mind." The emphasis is on giving careful, attentive consideration. |

     *Appropriate Thought*     *Opposite*

A.

B.

C.

D.

E.

F.

2. What two words did Paul use to summarize the six qualities of an appropriate thought life? (v. 8)

3. What actions or experiences contribute to building a proper thought life?

| Explaining the Text | Examining the Text |
|---|---|
| | What actions or experiences encourage improper thoughts? |
| 4. Though specific instruction is a helpful starting point, Paul recognized the importance of general guidance and example in helping believers know how to live in a way that pleases God. | 4. What was the relationship between Paul's life and the practical everyday lives of those whom he had taught? (v. 9) |
| | 5. What should a teacher expect from students after the lesson has been taught? (v. 9) |
| | 6. When Christians act in the way that Paul challenged them to, how will God minister to them? (v. 9) |

B. FEELING SPIRITUAL CONTENTMENT (*Phil. 4:10-13*). One of the goals of much current advertising is to encourage us to be discontent with what we have. There always is something newer or better. And yet a key quality of the Christian life is contentment. As Christians, we need to recognize that happiness is not determined by our circumstances.

| Explaining the Text | Examining the Text |
|---|---|
| 1. The Philippians had expressed their concern for Paul by sending a gift that was delivered by Epaphroditus (Phil. 4:18; cp. 2:25). | 1. What was the reason for Paul's ability to rejoice? (v. 10) |

| *Examining the Text* | *Explaining the Text* |
|---|---|
| 2. What tension had the Philippians experienced in helping to provide for Paul's needs while he was under house arrest? (v. 10) | 2. Apparently Paul had been in need for some time before the gift arrived. Paul's comments in verse 10 were meant to summarize his situation, *not* to criticize the Philippians' actions. |
| 3. From verse 12, list the extreme circumstances Paul had experienced during his life. | 3. For a more complete listing of the hardships Paul had experienced, read 2 Corinthians 11:23-28. |
| 4. To what extent did the circumstances in which Paul found himself determine how he felt and how he responded? (v. 11) | |
| 5. What was the secret of Paul's ability to live above his circumstances? (v. 13) | |
| 6. What is the difference between Paul's attitude toward his circumstances and the Stoic philosophy of refusing to admit either pleasure or pain? | 6. Some have suggested that Paul followed the Stoics. But the Stoics were more fatalistic and individualistic (they claimed to need no one). The Stoics practiced in rigid self-control, refusing to admit that they cared for pain or pleasure. |

C. SHOWING SPIRITUAL GENEROSITY (*Phil. 4:14-19*). It is very easy to forget when people do nice things for us. But Paul was able to recount each of the times that the Philippians had given to him. And he reminded them how their gifts pleased God.

*Explaining the Text*

1. The events that Paul referred to are recorded in Acts 16:10 and 17:1.

*Examining the Text*

1. When had the Philippians sent gifts to Paul to help supply his physical needs?

    *A.* (v. 15)

    *B.* (v. 16)

    *C.* (v. 18)

2. To what extent did the Philippians help Paul when he had need in Thessalonica? (v. 16)

3. Paul did not maintain that he didn't need the gift. He already had expressed that need. But his desire had more to do with the Philippians' benefit than his own.

3. What are the two benefits that come from meeting the physical needs of a fellow believer? (v. 17)

4. How did God view the gifts sent by the Philippians? (v. 18)

5. Verse 19 expresses one consequence of giving; it does not suggest the motivation for giving.

5. What can we expect to happen when we share our physical resources to help meet the needs of others? (v. 19)

D. CONCLUSION AND FINAL WORDS (*Phil. 4:20-23*). It is obvious, even in the way that he closed his letter, that Paul had deep affection for the Philippians.

| Examining the Text | Explaining the Text |
|---|---|
| 1. How does Paul's concluding statement tie into his original prayer for the Philippians? (v. 20; cp. 1:9-11) | |
| 2. What do you think Paul meant when he expressed a desire that glory be to God forever? (v. 20) | |
| 3. How does it encourage you to hear from fellow Christians whom God has been blessing? (vv. 21-22) | 3. The word *saint* (*haggios*, "set apart" or "sacred") refers to anyone or anything specifically set apart to God. It is used in verses 21-22 to refer to believers—followers of Jesus Christ. "Brothers" (v. 21) possibly refers to specific individuals, such as Timothy and Epaphroditus. |
| 4. What special group of saints sent their specific greetings via Paul? (v. 22) | 4. "Those who belong to Caesar's household" probably refers to guards assigned to Paul whom he had led to faith in Christ. |

*Experiencing the Text*

1. Evaluate how you spend your work and your leisure time. Do the things that you focus on (during both of these times) meet the six criteria of the kinds of things that we should think about?

   How do your reading, viewing, and listening habits need to change in order to help you focus on things that are "excellent" and "praiseworthy"?

2. List some of the difficult circumstances that you have faced (or will face) in your life.


What difference does it make to you that you have a source of power to draw on that enables you to cope with such pressures?


3. What resources do you have to share with those in need? What individuals or groups need some tangible expression of your (spiritual) love and concern for them?


What steps are you going to take in order to meet those needs?

# Introduction to the Epistles to the Colossians and Philemon

Colossians and Philemon both are Prison Epistles. That is, they were written by Paul while he was under house arrest at Rome. Thcy probably were written around A.D. 60. Tychicus, who delivered the Ephesian letter, may also have delivered the Epistles to the Colossians and Philemon.

The city of Colosse was one of the major cities in the Lycus Valley, located about 100 miles east of Ephesus. It was a sophisticated, cosmopolitan city, but avoided many of the excesses characteristic of seaports. It was surrounded by productive pastures, and the land contained valuable minerals. It's probable that Paul never visited Colosse.

The occasion for writing was to correct theological error that had begun to dominate the church. From what we read in the epistle, false teachers were taking what they had learned from Paul and others, reinterpreting it, and then adding their own erroneous teachings. One key error seems to have had a Jewish influence. Apparently, some were taking various elements from the Mosaic Law, rabbinic Judaism, and Christianity, and blending them all together.

Another error stressed that only those with special insight (*gnosis* or wisdom) were able to really understand the Christian religion. In this mix, Greek philosophy and Eastern mysticism were corrupting the pure Christian belief. Obviously, those who claimed special insight were the self-proclaimed teachers.

Perhaps the greatest error centered around the person of Christ. This heresy, an early form of gnosticism, proclaimed that pure spirit was good and matter (the material world) was evil. Between pure spirit and matter was a continuum with Jesus at the top (but below God) followed by other spiritual beings (angels or demigods) and finally humankind (because of our physical bodies) at the bottom. These early gnostics advocated the worship of angels and believed that one must progress up the ladder in order to get to God. For this reason, the person and work of Christ comprise the major emphases of Colossians.

Philemon, written at about the same time, was addressed to a believer at Colosse. It shows Christianity's intensely practical dimension—how it can make a difference in a believer's life. I pray that as you study these two books, you will gain a new, fuller understanding of Jesus Christ, and the difference He makes in our lives.

# Colossians 1:1-20

## Who Is Jesus Christ?

Recently I was reviewing a journal that I kept on a ministry trip to India. This was my first experience in a non-Western, non-European culture. And it is obvious from my journal entries that the transition was more demanding than I had expected.

Just getting to India was a chore; Delhi is just short of halfway around the world from Chicago. We left Chicago at 6:00 P.M. Sunday, with a four-hour layover in Amsterdam, and finally arrived in Delhi early Tuesday morning. After a few hours of sleep, the next leg of my journey took me down to Bangalore.

By the time my host and I finished meeting people, touring Bangalore, and ministering in a variety of contexts, I was suffering from information overload. It was exciting but very demanding. And then we hurried to the airport for the flight from Bangalore to Hyderabad, thinking that we didn't have much time. But we were mistaken. We had hours to wait, hours with no electricity, no air conditioning, and swarms of mosquitoes. The constant blare of sitar music (unlike any music I ever had heard) and the "meal" in the terminal added to my feeling of strangeness.

Finally, after hours of delay, we took off and eventually arrived at Hyderabad. But shortly after arriving I realized I had lost the tickets for all my remaining flights in India and the return trip to the U.S. My mind was a jumble of questions: "Why me?" "What next?" "Can I survive this?" And at that particular moment I found very few answers. But within a few hours I was able to call back to the States to talk with Elaine, my wife. And somehow that made all the difference in the world.

The Apostle Paul's letter of hope, encouragement, and instruction was probably even more welcome than my telephone conversation with Elaine. The Colossians were struggling to evaluate their world from a Christian point of view. And to the thirsty Colossians, this letter was a cup of spiritual cold water.

A. INTRODUCTION AND THANKSGIVING FOR THE COLOSSIANS (*Col. 1:1-8*). If you have ever been separated for a long time from someone you love, you have a small sense of what Paul felt. Though he may never have met most of the Colossian believers, Paul was vitally concerned for their welfare, and prayed for them regularly.

*Examining the Text*

*Explaining the Text*

1. Read Colossians 1:1-8. Who were the two people sending this epistle (letter)? (v. 1)

*Paul and Timothy*

1. Rather than ending a letter with the name of the sender (as we do today), in biblical times, the sender usually listed his name first.

2. Who were the recipients of the letter? (v. 2)

*Brothers in Colosse*

2. "Brothers" was probably a generic term that Paul used to address all of the believers at Colosse, not just the men.

How did Paul describe them? (v. 2)

*Saints*
*Faithful*

3. Why do you think that Paul stressed grace and peace at the beginning of almost all of his epistles? (v. 2)

4. What was an important part of Paul's prayer for the Colossians? (v. 3) *Give thanks to God, the Father and the Lord Jesus for them.*

4. Even though Paul had probably never visited the church at Colosse (1:7; 2:1), he still felt a keen sense of responsibility for this group of young believers.

5. How often do you think Paul prayed for the Christians in the church at Colosse? (v. 3)

*Praying, always for you.*

*Explaining the Text*

6. Notice the flow of verses 3-8. Paul was thankful for faith and love (v. 4), which sprang from hope (v. 5), based on the truth taught (v. 5), which produced fruit (v. 6).

8. Epaphras apparently helped to start the church at Colosse (4:12). The name Epaphras may be a short form of the name Epaphroditus (cp. Philippians 2:25-30).

*Examining the Text*

6. What two traits found among the Colossian believers was Paul thankful for? (v. 4)

Faith in Christ Jesus
Love for all the saints

7. What is the source of faith and love? (v. 5)

Because of the hope which is laid up in heaven.

8. What seems to be the relationship between "truth" and the Gospel (vv. 5-6) that was taught by Epaphras?

9. What can you say about Epaphras based on Paul's comments about him in verses 7-8?

Faithful minister of Christ.

B. PRAYER FOR KNOWLEDGE AND RIGHTEOUS BEHAVIOR (*Col. 1:9-14*). You've probably heard someone comment about another person: "He knew better than to do something like that!" or "When is he ever going to learn?" Inherent in these statements is the idea that we should relate knowledge to behavior. Paul is saying something similar in this passage: We need to know certain truths; then we need to put them into practice.

*Explaining the Text*

1. "Have not stopped praying" does not necessarily mean Paul prayed constantly. More likely, it indicates that Paul remembered them *regularly*, whenever he prayed.

*Examining the Text*

1. Read Colossians 1:9-14. When did Paul begin praying for the Colossian believers? (v. 9)

*Examining the Text*

2. What are some of the specific things that Paul prayed for? (v. 9) Filled with the Knowledge of His Will All wisdom & spiritual under-standing

What do you think this meant?
We are to know who Christ is by His Knowledge and wisdom

3. What is the purpose of being filled with knowledge? (v. 10) That you may walk a life worthy of the Lord.

4. In verses 10-12, Paul described four components of living a life that is worthy of the Lord and pleasing to Him. What are these components?

A. (v. 10) Fully pleasing Him Fruitful in every good work

B. (v. 10) Increasing in the Knowledge of God.

C. (v. 11) Strengthened with all might. for all patience, long suffering with joy

D. (v. 12) Giving thanks to the Father.

Evaluate your life in regard to each of these four categories. In which of the categories do you see the most progress?

In which category do you need to grow through God's help? All.

*Explaining the Text*

2. "Spiritual wisdom" refers to the practical application of knowledge. "Understanding" implies clear evaluation and decision-making.

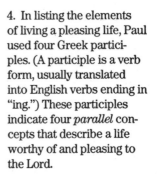

4. In listing the elements of living a pleasing life, Paul used four Greek participles. (A participle is a verb form, usually translated into English verbs ending in "ing.") These participles indicate four *parallel* concepts that describe a life worthy of and pleasing to the Lord.

*Explaining the Text*

5. Verses 12-13 contrast two power systems—the kingdom of light (the church under Christ's power, v. 12), and the dominion of darkness (the world system under Satan's power, v. 13).

*Examining the Text*

5. How does it encourage us to know that we have been rescued from Satan's dominion and now are under Christ's dominion? (v. 13)

6. What has Christ done to qualify us to be participants in His kingdom? (v. 14)

*In whom we have redemption Through His blood, the forgiveness of sins.*

C. THE PLACE AND POSITION OF CHRIST (*Col. 1:15-20*). Since Jesus Christ is the head of the kingdom of light, it is important to understand His qualifications for this position. In this section, Paul clearly presents Christ's credentials—*who* He is and *what* He has done.

*Explaining the Text*

1."Firstborn" (v. 15) describes a position of authority and privilege; it does not imply that Jesus is part of God's creation. This is clear from the phrase "before all things" (v. 17), which suggests that Christ is fully God, not created.

*Examining the Text*

1. Read Colossians 1:15-20. Paul described seven key characteristics of Jesus. List the seven characteristics and what each means to you. (Note: For a fuller analysis of this section, see the *Bible Knowledge Commentary, N.T.*, Victor, pp. 672–674).

  *A.* (v. 15) *He is the Image of the invisible God - r*

  *B.* (v. 15) *First born of all creation.*

  *C.* (v. 16) *All things created by Him*

  *D.* (v. 18) *Head of the body, the Church.*

  *E.* (v. 18) *Beginning of the first born from the dead*

## Examining the Text

F. (v. 19) *It pleased the Father that in Him all the fulness shall dwell.*

G. (v. 20) *He reconciled all things to Himself.*

2. We are alienated from God by our sin. By what means can we be reconciled to God? (v. 20)

*Through the <u>blood</u> of His cross.*

3. What are the practical implications for Christians' relationships because of reconciliation to Christ? (v. 20)

## Explaining the Text

## Experiencing the Text

1. How should we feel about Christians (especially young Christians) who are in the process of growing?

2. Make a list of some ways you could stimulate young Christians to further growth.

3. Make a list of activities (or projects) that would help you to:

Bear fruit,

Grow in the knowledge of God,

Be strengthened so that you have endurance and patience,

Give thanks joyfully.

Choose one of these activities and develop a plan to carry it out. Before you begin, ask God to grant you spiritual wisdom and understanding to know how to proceed.

# Colossians 1:21–2:5

## What Difference Does Christ Make?

I continue to be amazed at the gullibility of people generally, and of Americans specifically. An evening of watching television should lay to rest any illusions that we are a critical and discerning people. Abundant commercial messages range in appeal from sophisticated and subtle to insulting and demeaning; yet we continue to watch, and apparently we purchase the products advertised.

But the sponsors of television shows do not have a corner on the inane. Recently my wife showed me an unbelievable magazine advertisement of a woman emotionally distressed because her husband was losing interest in her. The underlying cause of his imminent abandonment was the water spots left on the drinking glasses by *her* automatic dishwasher!

Recently I was reminded of my own gullibility as I used a duffel bag that I had purchased based on a printed ad. I had read in the advertisement that this particular item was a "World Famous" duffel bag. Thinking that it obviously had been manufactured by a company that I knew and respected, I decided to order the product. And when it arrived, we saw that indeed it was as the ad indicated. It was manufactured by the World Famous Company, Taiwan.

The same principle applies to truth. It seems as though whatever is beautiful and valuable will have its false counterpart. This began in the Garden of Eden when Satan offered a counterfeit alternative to God's plan. It was true in the life and ministry of Paul. Even as Paul was teaching about who Christ is and what He did, false teachers were promoting subtle distortions. This passage presents truth about Christ so that the Colossians (and we) could discern error and cling firmly to the truth. Let's not be duped!

A. WE HAVE BEEN RECONCILED TO CHRIST (*Col 1:21-23*). If two people have been arguing, we often admonish them to make up—to be reconciled to each other. Both must be restored. However, in the spiritual realm, we must be reconciled to God. We must make the change, not God.

| *Examining the Text* | *Explaining the Text* |
|---|---|
| 1. Read Colossians 1:21-23. What is the relationship of a nonbeliever to God? (v. 21) | 1. Paul chose to use a before/after description to explain what happens when a person becomes a Christian. |

*Alienated and enemies in your mind*

What caused this relationship? (v. 21)

*Wicked works.*

2. What new standing do we have before God because of being reconciled? (v. 22)

*In the body of His flesh through death: to present you holy and blameless; and irreproachable in His sight*

2. As unbelievers we were alienated from God before we become Christians. Therefore, we needed to be reconciled. This means that we were brought into a relationship with God that was not possible before we received forgiveness of sins through the death of Christ

3. What is the means by which reconciliation was accomplished? (v. 22)

*In the body (of Christ) His flesh through death.*

3. The heretical teaching at Colosse (an early form of Gnosticism) denied both the deity and the humanity of Christ. Paul dealt with each topic in this epistle.

4. What are the characteristics of a believer who continues in the faith? (v. 23)

*Grounded and steadfast Are not moved away from the hope of the gospel*

4. In verse 23, the Greek language structure indicates that Paul had no question about the believers continuing. It could be translated "since you continue."

*Explaining the Text*

5. "To every creature under heaven" describes the universality of the Gospel, and the fact that Christ has brought it to everyone (cp. 1 Peter 3:18-19).

*Examining the Text*

5. What is the means that God has chosen for the Gospel to be proclaimed everywhere? (v. 23)

*To be preached to every creatures. under the heavens.*

6. How did Paul view himself, and how can this be an example to us? (v. 23) *As a minister*

*We are to be ministers - priests Set apart to Him.*

---

B. CHRIST MAKES A DIFFERENCE IN OUR LIVES (*Col. 1:24-27*). God has revealed many things through His Word, but He did not reveal them all at exactly the same time. One of His later revelations was made through Jesus Christ: through Him, all believers have been united in one body, the church.

*Explaining the Text*

1. Apparently, even as Christ suffered in paying the price for our salvation, others also can expect to experience suffering in bringing the Gospel to those who may not have heard.

*Examining the Text*

1. Read Colossians 1:24-27. In what ways might Paul, through his own suffering, have contributed to building up the church, Christ's body? (v. 24)

How might we make similar contributions?

2. Who commissioned Paul as a servant? (v. 25)

*Examining the Text*

    What is the job of a person who is a servant of the Gospel? (v. 25)

3. How does the mystery (v. 26) affect those who are Gentiles (non-Jews)? (v. 27)

4. What actually is the content of the mystery? (v. 27)

    How does it affect the way that we view the future? (v. 27)

*Explaining the Text*

3. In Paul's writing he often speaks of a "mystery." This refers to truth not known in the past that has been revealed by God for Paul to share through his teaching.

4. "Hope of glory" anticipates the future and focuses on what we can expect to experience as believers—members of the church, the body of Christ.

C. WE ARE COMPLETE IN CHRIST (*Col. 1:28-29*). Each of us has something that is the driving force in our lives. Paul's drive was twofold. He wanted to bring as many to Christ as possible. And then he wanted them to come to full maturity.

*Examining the Text*

1. Read Colossians 1:28-29. What is involved in proclaiming (telling others about) Christ? (v. 28)

*Explaining the Text*

| Explaining the Text | Examining the Text |
|---|---|
| 2. "Perfect" could most accurately be translated by a word such as "complete" or "mature." | 2. What is the objective (or goal) of this proclamation? (v. 28) |
| 3. Perhaps Paul worked so hard because of the magnitude of the task he faced. His goal was that everyone in the entire world would hear about Christ. | 3. With what attitude and in what way did Paul proclaim the Gospel? (v. 29) |
| | 4. Whose energy inspired and energized Paul? (v. 29) |
| | 5. In what way did the source of Paul's energy make a difference in the way that Paul served God? (v. 29) |

D. WE HAVE STABILITY IN CHRIST ALONE (*Col. 2:1-5*). One heretical teaching which Paul was confronting in this passage rejected the truth about the person and work of Christ, and replaced it with philosophical human speculation. The clarifying message of Colossians is just as relevant today as when it was written.

| Explaining the Text | Examining the Text |
|---|---|
| 1. Apparently the heresy that Paul was combating had spread from Colosse to other cities in the Lycus Valley, including Laodicea. | 1. Read Colossians 2:1-5. How could Paul have been struggling so about those whom he had never even met personally? (v. 1) |

| Examining the Text | Explaining the Text |
|---|---|
| 2. What was Paul's purpose in his struggle for the Colossians (and the Laodiceans)? (v. 2) | |
| 3. What two conditions in a Christian's life will lead to the full riches of complete understanding? (v. 2) | 3. Apparently heart attitude (proper relationship to Christ) enables a Christian's mind to function more effectively. |
| 4. What is the ultimate source of truth? (vv. 2-3) | 4. Regardless of how impressive any argument may sound, if it contradicts God's revealed truth, it is false. |
| 5. Contrast what we have in Christ (v. 3) with what is delivered by those offering alternatives (v. 4). | 5. Since Christ is the creator and the sustainer of the universe (1:15-17), He obviously is not lacking in any knowledge. In addition, all of God's fullness resides in Him too (1:19). |
| 6. What alternatives had been proposed to the believers at Colosse? (v. 4) | |
| 7. How might we face similar confrontation with alternatives today? | 7. Virtually all cults and false religions reject or distort revealed truth about the person and work of Christ. |
| 8. What was a source of great delight as Paul reviewed the ministry that he had shared with the Colossians? (v. 5) | |

*Experiencing the Text*

1. What are some of the changes that have taken place in your life since you were reconciled to God through faith in the work of Christ?

   In what areas do you presently see some progress, or do you need to see progress?

2. What does it mean to us today (as individuals and as groups of Christians) to know that we are part of Christ's body, and that His Spirit lives in us?

3. How can Paul's example of diligence as he served Christ influence us in the way that we serve Him today?

4. What are some false teachings about the person or the work of Christ that we might encounter today?

   How can we prepare ourselves to discern and respond to false teaching?

# Colossians 2:6-23

## Christ Frees Us from Empty Religion

Recently I was talking with a surgeon friend about attitudes that people have toward illness, and specifically the way they view terminal illness. Some come to grips with the reality of the situation and face their future with a quiet confidence in God. But others have a very different perspective. These people grasp desperately at any strand of hope, however remote the possibility of recovery. In some cases, the more remote the possibility of cure, the more tenaciously they cling to unrealistic hope. There may be nothing that they can do; yet they seem driven to do something—anything—just to be doing.

I suppose that this is a fairly common reaction. We seem to feel better doing something, even if down deep we know that there is nothing to do. Perhaps we feel that if we only try harder, or do more, we'll get the results we want.

Not long ago I was driving to the airport with a coworker. As we neared the airport, we had to cross railroad tracks. And as always seems to be the case when we are in a hurry, there was a train blocking the crossing. As soon as I realized what was happening, I made a U-turn and wound around the back streets trying to find a better way across the tracks. But the train was going the same direction as we, and so I wound up waiting at another crossing farther along the tracks.

I found myself explaining that we probably didn't gain any time, but at least I felt as though I was doing something, which made me feel better than just sitting in traffic waiting for the train to clear the crossing. And we did arrive in time to make our flight anyway.

We may understand people who desperately struggle with grief, and we may forgive compulsive drivers trying to gain an edge. But often people carry the same attitude into Christian living. They want to work to earn something—to do it themselves. Not only is such an attitude deceptively useless, but it actually can hinder true spiritual growth.

A. FREE TO LIVE BY FAITH (*Col. 2:6-8*). When a person learns a new skill, he or she usually is careful to follow proper procedures. But over time, carelessness may set in and bad habits may proliferate. With this tendency in mind, Paul admonished the Colossians to remember to continue living by faith, even as they had started.

| *Examining the Text* | *Explaining the Text* |
|---|---|
| 1. Read Colossians 2:6-8. What is the way in which we should live in Christ? (v. 6) | |
| 2. In what way is "rooted" a good description of the Christian life? (v. 6) | 2. The words "rooted" and "built up" provide us with concrete illustrations of the Christian life. |
| How does "built up" illustrate another aspect of the Christian life? (v. 6) | |
| 3. What was the basic teaching that strengthened the Colossian believers? (v. 7) | |
| 4. What can be the result of philosophical thinking that is not grounded in the revealed truth of God? (v. 8) | 4. "Hollow" can mean empty or not real, pretentious, worthless. "Deceptive" is something that would misrepresent or cheat. |
| 5. What is the basis of "hollow" or "deceptive" philosophizing? (v. 8) | |

| *Explaining the Text* | *Examining the Text* |
|---|---|
| | And what did Paul suggest as an alternative? (v. 8) |

B. FREE FROM THE CURSE OF LEGALISM (*Col. 2:9-15*). The Mosaic Law was a gracious gift from God. It freed Israel to serve God intelligently. David exclaimed, "Oh, how I love Your law! I meditate on it all day long" (Ps. 119:97). And yet it also presented an absolute standard—unattainable and condemning. Christ freed us from this, and Paul did not want believers to be placed back under it.

| *Explaining the Text* | *Examining the Text* |
|---|---|
| | 1. Read Colossians 2:9-15. How does the essential nature of Christ contrast with philosophical speculation? (vv. 9-10) |
| 2. One of the key tenets of Gnosticism was that Christ was neither totally God nor totally man. Rather they claimed that He was an intermediate step, less than God, but more than man. | 2. How do verses 9-10 directly confront and answer the Gnostic heresy? |
| | 3. What have we believers actually received in Christ? (v. 10) |
| 4. For Israel, physical circumcision was the sign of identification to show their relationship with God. Spiritually we are identified with Christ, and our "cutting off" is a break with the past. | 4. What happened to our sinful natures when we accepted Christ? (v. 11) |

| Examining the Text | Explaining the Text |
|---|---|
| 5. How is baptism a picture of what happened to us as we entered our new relationships with Christ at salvation? (v. 12) | 5. The baptism pictured here seems to be immersion, as in Jewish proselyte baptism. |
| 6. Contrast a believer's condition before and after salvation (v. 13).<br>      *Before*                    *After* | |
| 7. What did Christ do to the Law and to the power of sin through His death? (vv. 14-15) | 7. The "written code" refers to the Mosaic Law which specified God's absolute standards and showed Israel how far short they fell of those standards. Christ not only obeyed all the Law perfectly, but triumphed over its penalty through His death and resurrection. |

C. FREE FROM RELIGIOUS SPECULATION (*Col. 2:16-19*). It seems as if anyone can get a platform from which to speak. Sometimes it's those with the least to say (but who say it loudly) that people begin to believe. The phenomenon is not new. It happened in Paul's day. And the contrived religion was worthless, although it was persuasive-sounding.

| Examining the Text | Explaining the Text |
|---|---|
| 1. Read Colossians 2:16-19. What was the relationship between the Mosaic Law and Christ? (vv. 16-17) | 1. The items mentioned in verse 16 are regulations that were included as part of the Mosaic Law Sab- |

| *Explaining the Text* | *Examining the Text* |
|---|---|
| bath (Saturday) worship was under Law. Christians changed the worship day to Sunday in recognition of Christ's resurrection. | |
| | 2. How is the illustration of a shadow appropriate to describe the Law and the relationship that it bore to Christ? (v. 17) |
| 3. The Gnostic heresy claimed that Jesus was less than God, and angels were less than Jesus but greater than humans. The Gnostics taught that the angels should be worshiped with Christ. | 3. What trap have those people fallen into who contrive religious regulations? (v. 18) |
| | 4. What would be the consequence of their fallacious system? (v. 18) |
| | What do you think "the prize" is that Paul referred to? (v. 18) |
| 5. Paul pictured the Church as a growing body, with each part having special, unique functions to provide (see 1 Corinthians 12:12-26). All parts are important because all of the functions are necessary. | 5. Who is the Head of the body? (v. 19) |
| | What role does the Head play? |

D. FREE FROM USELESS RESTRICTION (*Col. 2:20-23*). Many Christians seem to feel that leading very restrictive lives and watching their behavior carefully will keep them close to Christ. But instead they can be lulled into a false sense of complacency. Rigid lifestyle doesn't deal with physical drives that can lead into sin.

| *Examining the Text* | *Explaining the Text* |
|---|---|
| 1. Read Colossians 2:20-23. What are the characteristics of a restrictive lifestyle that focuses on what a person doesn't do? (v. 21) | |
| 2. What kinds of principles does this type of approach rely on? (v. 22) | 2. Rigid restrictions, as when Israel was under the Mosaic Law, never can draw people close to God. They could not produce spirituality then and cannot today either. |
| 3. What is the reason that we don't need to be obligated to a negative religion? (v. 20) | 3. Since we died with Christ (Col. 2:12) believers have been freed to new spiritual motivation and victorious living in Christ. |
| 4. What are the categories that those who present a negative religion focus on? (v. 23) | |
| 5. What does religious negativism accomplish? (v. 23)<br><br>What does it fail to accomplish? (v. 23) | 5. While there is nothing inherently wrong with a rigid, restrictive code of behavior, we should recognize that it does nothing to deal with our underlying drives that still encourage us to sin. |

*Experiencing the Text*

1. In what ways is your life different because of your relationship with Jesus Christ? How does He influence your values and the way that you look at life?

2. How do you feel when you know that the power of God, who raised Jesus Christ from the dead, dwells within you?

3. How could a false, contrived religious system hinder you from living a dynamic Christian life?

What can we do to make sure that we don't substitute empty religious ritual for a true, vital relationship with Christ?

4. How can we set appropriate behavior guidelines for ourselves while at the same time avoiding narrow religious negativism that is worthless for building true Christian character?

# Colossians 3:1-17

## How to Lead a Holy Life

At one time or another all of us have tried to change some habit that we didn't like. For most of us, we found the *decision* to change that habit an easy one to make. But when it came time to *follow through*—to put up or shut up—well, that's another story.

One young woman began to smoke cigarettes as a teenager. And by the time she was in her twenties, smoking was a well-established habit. But she hated the fact that she smoked. One day I asked her if she had ever thought about quitting. She looked at me incredulously and replied, "Every single morning of my life!"

Of course she had developed a physiological addiction. But in addition to that, smoking had become a habit. It was something that she did without thinking. By definition, a habit is something that we do unconsciously—never actually choosing that particular action. And by experience, it is something that is extremely compelling.

Most of us have established ingrained eating habits that we slavishly pursue. But one day we discover that for a particular reason we need to change the pattern. Eggs are high in cholesterol. Salty french fries ooze saturated fat. Our active lifestyles have become settled, and suddenly many of the calories we ingest also are settling—in obvious places.

And so we decide to change eating habits. But it is very difficult to reduce intake or cut out favorite foods. Rather we must establish new habit patterns—replace old habits with new. And the same thing is true in living the Christian life. Paul warned against superficial religion that focuses on the "don'ts." In this section he explains how we can replace the negatives with positive alternatives. New habits force out the old. Vital Christian living replaces meaningless negativism.

A. FOCUS ON SPIRITUAL VALUES (*Col. 3:1-4*). We are built in such a way that it's almost impossible to concentrate on not thinking about something. If you are on a diet and you concentrate on not thinking about a hot fudge sundae you soon will crave it. In this passage Paul suggests that rather than trying to concentrate on not doing things, we should set our minds on spiritual things—things above.

| *Examining the Text* | *Explaining the Text* |
|---|---|
| 1. Read Colossians 3:1-4. What is the reason that we should focus on things above? (v. 1) | 1. This section presents a positive alternative to the rigid negativism of the preceding section. |
| 2. What do you think is the main emphasis of setting our "hearts" on things above? (v. 1) | 2. The expression "set your hearts/minds" both emphasize intense seeking or concentration. |
| 3. What do you think is the main emphasis of setting our "minds" on things above? (v. 2) | |
| 4. How is positively focusing on spiritual values better than concentrating on trying to stop doing earthly things? | 4. "Earthly things" are in contrast with "things above." The contrast is physical/spiritual, temporary/eternal. |
| 5. How does our relationship with Christ affect the way we live right now? (v. 3) | 5. Christianity does not deal only with the present or only with the future. It brings both into focus, and enables us to live appropriately both here and now and also in eternity. |
| How will it affect the future? (v. 4) | |

| Explaining the Text | Examining the Text |
|---|---|
| | 6. What is Christ to us right now? (v. 4) |
| | How does this affect our thought/value system? |

B. PUT AWAY SINFUL BEHAVIOR (*Col. 3:5-11*). Even though in an earlier section of the book Paul admonished the Colossians not to focus all of their attention on earthly matters, behavior is important. And it is especially important for believers who have set their hearts and minds on things above. We need to stop our old sinful ways.

| Explaining the Text | Examining the Text |
|---|---|
| 1. Instead of following the dictates of our sinful (earthly) natures, we have been freed to respond as Christ directs. | 1. Read Colossians 3:5-11. What does "therefore" suggest to the reader? (v. 5) |
| | How do our new relationships with Christ (vv. 1-4) influence putting to death our earthly natures? (v. 5) |
| 2. Paul is not suggesting that we avoid material things. But behavior that is motivated only by our earthly natures will contradict what is appropriate to a believer. | 2. What behavior characteristics grow out of our earthly natures? (v. 5) |
| | 3. What will happen to those who are driven by their earthly natures, and whose lives are characterized by sinful behavior? (v. 6) |

| Examining the Text | Explaining the Text |
|---|---|
| 4. List characteristics of earthly behavior (vv. 8-9) and then contrast what is appropriate behavior for a Christian.<br><br>*OLD BEHAVIOR*          *NEW BEHAVIOR* | 4. While philosophical religious speculation makes a person seem wise, it does nothing to change the behavior of an individual. When we have been seated with Christ and focus our attention on things above (v. 2), then we receive God's power to actually change our behavior. |
| 5. Describe the kind of people that we are becoming based on the work of God in our lives (vv. 9-10). | |
| 6. What does Christ do to eradicate those differences that are so important to us on earth? (v. 11)<br><br>What does this imply about our attitudes and responses to those who may be different from us? | 6. The barriers that are broken down are religious, national, cultural, and social. Even though our earthly natures set up barriers, Christ breaks them down and binds us together in His body, the church. |

C. PRACTICE SPIRITUAL BEHAVIOR (*Col. 3:12-17*). Whenever there is a vacuum, it tends to be filled. And the same is true in our personal lives. Just eliminating behavior does not solve our behavior problem. Eliminated behavior must be replaced by the correct kind—behavior that glorifies God, that is appropriate to believers.

## Explaining the Text

1. Christianity is not some vague, abstract concept. Rather, it is a new relationship with God through Jesus Christ. God gives us new minds and a new source of power that enables us to behave in a godly manner. Rather than just a list of things that we cannot do, following Christ involves our entire lifestyles, with the power provided to enable us to live in the way that God expects us to live. It is intensely practical.

## Examining the Text

1. Read Colossians 3:12-17. List the characteristics of a person demonstrating holy behavior as a chosen one of God, and then describe an example of how each quality can be shown in daily life.

GODLY PRACTICE          PRACTICAL EXAMPLE

A. (v. 12)

B. (v. 12)

C. (v. 12)

D. (v. 12)

E. (v. 12)

F. (v. 13)

G. (v. 14)

2. What should characterize relationships among believers? (v. 15)

3. "Word of Christ" refers to the revelation (the Bible) that includes, but probably is not limited to, Christ's earthly conversation. "Teaching" means giving instruction; "admonishing" is challenging or exhorting.

3. How should we minister to each other? (v. 16)

| Examining the Text | Explaining the Text |
|---|---|
| 4. What should be our attitude toward God? (v. 17) | 4. It is very easy to talk one style of behavior and live another. Both words and actions need to be guided by the same principles. What we say and what we do should correspond with each other. |

## Experiencing the Text

1. In what way might our recreational and entertainment preferences indicate the focus of our minds and hearts?

    What changes might be appropriate in your vocational, recreational, and entertainment activities if you were to focus your heart and mind more fully on things above?

2. What are some of the human, earthly barriers to godly relationships that Christ needs to remove so that you can demonstrate proper attitudes toward others?

3. Reread Colossians 3:15-17. Write a paragraph describing how your church might come to a decision about how to use a large sum of money willed to you by a deceased member. (Assume that your church is actively practicing the principles described in verses 15-17.)

# Colossians 3:18–4:18

## How to Get Along with Others

A little more than a year ago we had a late spring ice storm. And as is often the case in ice storms, our electric service was disrupted. It was amazing to see how incapacitated we were when all of a sudden we had to try to function without electricity. We spent hours just caring for the mundane tasks of living.

We and our neighbors marveled at how we take for granted something that we depend on so greatly. Walking over to a wall switch and flicking on the light has become second nature. So much so that several times I felt quite foolish for trying to turn on a light when I knew there was no electricity.

My experience was not all that unique. It revealed a very human characteristic. We take for granted those things with which we are most familiar. The first time that we encounter something new, we may stand in awe, overcome with amazement. And yet in no time at all we come to accept this marvelous innovation—never even giving it a second thought. And only when we have to do without do we gain a renewed appreciation for what we commonly accept.

The same is true in our relationships. We usually take for granted family and friends whom we contact every day. And only as we are separated do we realize how significant those people are to us.

Paul demonstrated his deep love and appreciation for those whom he could not speak to in person. This last section of Colossians is an expression of a man who loved his fellow Christians very deeply. And yet due to his imprisonment, he was denied access to their fellowship. These final verses came from deep in Paul's heart, and reached deep into the hearts of the Colossian believers.

A. RELATING TO FAMILY AND COWORKERS (*Col. 3:18–4:1*). It often
has been observed that it is very easy for a person to project the image he
desires when out in public. But if you really want to know a person,
observe how he acts at home. The guidelines in this section describe
appropriate behavior for a Christian in various contexts.

| Examining the Text | Explaining the Text |
|---|---|
| 1. Read Colossians 3:18–4:1. What is the responsibility of a wife to her husband? (v. 18) | 1. Each of these instructions is given as part of a pair of guidelines. Notice that the key element in each of these pairs is reciprocal responsibility. None of us relates in a vacuum, but we must give and take in the relationship. |
| What is a husband's responsibility to his wife? (v. 19) | |
| 2. How are instruction to both husband and wife needed in order to keep balance in the relationship? | |
| How does being a Christian contribute to the success of this relationship? (v. 11) | |
| 3. What instructions did Paul give to children? (v. 20) | 3. It is helpful to remember that submission is the standard for all believers. Christ submitted to God; we submit to Christ and then to each other (cp. Eph. 5:21-33). |
| And what did he expect of parents? (v. 21) | |

*Explaining the Text*

*Examining the Text*

4. In the first century, slaves worked for other people. This situation would be somewhat similar to employees today who work in a specific job for a salary.

4. What is the standard for workers? (v. 22)

5. Obviously, all of the same guidelines for behavior apply to non-Christians. But since Paul was writing to believers, he added the elements of spiritual motivation and ultimate reward.

5. What is the reason for a Christian working whole-heartedly for an employer? (v. 23)

What ultimate difference does it make to a Christian worker? (vv. 24-25)

6. How should an employer treat workers? (4:1)

What are some reasons that Christian employers should act in this way? (v. 1)

B. RELATING TO NON-CHRISTIANS (*Col. 4:2-6*). Not only should believers relate properly to other members of the body of Christ, but we also need to build good relationships with unbelievers. We should look for ways to minister to them and to share God's Word.

| Examining the Text | Explaining the Text |
|---|---|
| 1. Read Colossians 4:2-6. What do we need in order to minister effectively? (v. 2) | 1. Apparently Paul was keenly aware of the fact that in and of himself he was insufficient for the magnitude of the task before him. |
| 2. What were some specific requests that Paul asked prayer for? (vv. 3-4) | 2. "In chains" probably refers to the fact that Paul was writing this epistle in Rome while under house arrest. |
| 3. How should we view relationships with outsiders? (vv. 4-6) | 3. "Outsiders" probably are those who are unbelievers, those outside of the body of Christ. |
| 4. What is the difference between being seasoned with salt and being salty? (v. 6)

How does "seasoned with salt" picture the quality of relationship that we should have with outsiders? | 4. Salt had two main functions in New Testament times. It was used as a flavor enhancer (as it is today); but more importantly it was used to preserve and retard spoilage since there were no chemical preservatives or refrigeration. |

C. RELATING TO OTHER BELIEVERS (*Col. 4:7-15*). "To live above with saints we love, oh, that will be glory. But to live below with saints we know—well, that's another story!" Unfortunately this may be true more often than we would like to admit. True Christianity should help believers get along better with each other.

| Explaining the Text | Examining the Text |
|---|---|
| 1. Tychicus was a co-worker of Paul (the carrier of the Epistle to the Colossians) and Onesimus was a runaway slave (the subject of the Epistle to Philemon). | 1. Read Colossians 4:7-15. What can we learn about Tychicus and Onesimus from this passage? (vv. 7-9) |
| | 2. How important is communication within the body of Christ? (vv. 7-9) |
| 3. Aristarchus and Mark both had accompanied Paul on certain of his missionary journeys. | 3. How important do you think coworkers were to the Apostle Paul? (vv. 7-15) |
| 4. Epaphras was a Colossian whom the church had sent to minister to Paul (cp. Col. 1:7). | 4. Describe what we know of Epaphras from this passage (vv. 12-13). |
| 5. Luke, the physician, was the author of the Gospel account bearing his name and also of the Acts of the Apostles, which contains the conclusion to the Gospel according to Luke | 5. How would you rate Paul as a minister and communicator, based on this passage?

What support can you find for such a conclusion? |

D. CONCLUSION (*Col. 4:16-18*). It was obvious from the final paragraphs of this letter that Paul deeply loved those to whom he had ministered. And yet when he finally reached the end of the letter, he ended rather abruptly, perhaps feeling great emotion

| Examining the Text | Explaining the Text |
|---|---|
| 1. Read Colossians 4:16-18. Why is it important for church leaders to make sure that Christians know and understand the contents of the Bible? (v. 16) | 1. The letter to the Laodiceans may be the Epistle to the Ephesians, or there may have been another letter written by Paul that is not included in the New Testament. |
| 2. What do you think was the background to the exhortation that Paul made to Archippus? (v. 17) | 2. Archippus may have been an interim pastor in the Colossian church while Epaphras, sent to minister to Paul in Rome, was absent. |
| 3. In what way could Paul's closing salutation to the Colossians be an inspiration to us? (v. 18) | 3. Paul probably dictated this letter (perhaps due to poor eyesight), but signed it personally to help authenticate the epistle. |

*Experiencing the Text*

1. In which of the sets of relationships (Col. 3:18–4:1) do you experience the greatest success in following the biblical guidelines?

2. In which of the sets of relationships do you experience the most difficulty?

What course of action can you suggest to help you strengthen those relationships?

3. What are some ways in which you have meaningful relationships with non-Christians?


Take some time right now and pray for those relationships, asking God to help you minister more effectively.


4. How is this record of Paul's attitude toward fellow workers an example for us today?


What can we do to cultivate similar attitudes toward our coworkers?

# Philemon

## Practical Christian Living

Have you ever noticed that there are some individuals who can inject "life" into a group of people—individuals who have that special gift? In the town where we used to live, Elaine and I had one friend who was just such a person. If we were planning a party, but weren't quite sure about the dynamics of the group, we would invite Bob. We knew that whenever Bob was there, everyone had a good time. He always had a good story that he could pull out at just the right moment. And Bob could tell a joke like no one you ever heard.

Often others of our friends would try to imitate Bob. They would tell his jokes, or try to recount his funny stories. Sometimes after a hilarious evening one of us would try to recount what happened for someone who wasn't there. But invariably the joke fell flat or the story became garbled. And the feeble attempt would be punctuated with "Well, you had to be there to appreciate it."

We found that there is a difference between knowing a joke and being able to tell a good joke. We discovered that the story was only a small part of Bob's secret. His real genius lay in being a person who loved people and had developed a skill for effective communication. It was his expertise that made the difference. All of us could grasp the theory of effective communication. But few had mastered his skill.

In many areas of life we understand principles, but are weak in practice. Unfortunately, one area where the gap between theory and practice often becomes a yawning chasm is in the application of spiritual principles.

At first glance, one might wonder why a book like Philemon—one chapter, twenty-five verses, written to one person—would be in the Bible. But it becomes obvious that it's a practical book that shows Christian love at work. It's a book we can understand and it guides us through Practical Christianity 101.

## A. INTRODUCTION AND PRAYER OF THANKSGIVING (*Phile. 1-7*).

When a person must be separated from loved ones, it is satisfying to hear that they are well and prospering. Paul thanked God that those of Philemon's house were thriving spiritually. And he prayed that this situation would continue.

*Examining the Text*

1. Read Philemon 1-7. Who were the persons sending this letter? (v. 1) *Paul + Timothy*

How did they describe themselves? (v. 1)
*Prisoners of Christ*

2. Who were the recipients of the letter and how did Paul describe each one? (vv. 1-2)
*Philemon — beloved friend & fellow laborer.*
*Apphia beloved*
*Archippus — fellow soldier.*

3. What conclusions can we draw about the kind of person Philemon was from the information in this section? (vv. 1-7) *He loved the Lord and all saints, He opened his home to the church. All the saints were refreshed by him.*

4. How did Paul seem to feel about Philemon? (vv. 1, 4, 7) *He feels he is a brother and always praying for Philemon. Has great joy and consolation in him because of love for all saints.*

5. In what ways is Philemon a good model for us to follow? *We should freely be committed — and to love our Lord and all saints. To be committed to the church giving all our love.*

*Explaining the Text*

1. Paul probably wrote this epistle while he was under house arrest in Rome. He seems to have written it at about the same time he wrote Colossians, and possibly Ephesians too (around A.D. 60).

2. Philemon probably was a wealthy Christian living in Colosse. Apphia may have been his wife and Archippus, his son.

3. The very fact that Philemon's home was appropriate for the church to meet in indicates something about his station in life.

4. Apparently Philemon had demonstrated an extraordinary level of commitment and ministry. Paul commended him for this attitude.

B. THE REASON FOR PAUL'S LETTER (*Phile. 8-16*). Although persons in positions of authority may have power, they don't have to wield it arbitrarily. Paul had full authority as an apostle, and yet he chose to ask Philemon, tactfully and graciously, for what he wanted.

*Explaining the Text*

1. Apparently Onesimus, Philemon's slave, had run away from Philemon to Rome. He may have met Paul there and become a Christian under Paul's ministry. Paul then sent him back to Philemon.

3. Onesimus was a common Greek name, especially for a slave. It meant "useful."

4. Perhaps Philemon had assisted Paul in one way or another. He may have contributed money or sent personal assistance.

*Examining the Text*

1. Read Philemon 8-16. How could Paul have approached Philemon, and what could he have demanded of him? (v. 8) *might Come in boldness of Christ to command you what is fitting*

2. What do you think "became my son" indicates about Onesimus? (v. 10) *Onesimus accepted Christ therefore Paul regarded him as a son*

3. How did Paul make a play on words describing Onesimus in relation to his name? (v. 11) *That he was once unprofitable but now profitable to him.*

4. What does it appear that Paul would have liked to do with Onesimus? (v. 13) *He wanted to keep Onesimus with him*

Instead, what did he choose to do? (v. 12) *He sent him back to Philemon.*

5. How did Paul feel about Onesimus? (vv. 12-13) *To recieve him as Paul did for he wanted to keep him for he ministered to him.*

*Examining the Text*

6. What response did Paul want from Philemon? (v. 14) *that his good deeds would not be by complusion but voluntary.*

*Explaining the Text*

7. How does Paul's description of the relationship between Philemon and Onesimus give insight into how the early church functioned? (vv. 15-16) *Philemon should recieve Onesimus as a brother instead of a slave.*

7. Even though there were obvious differences in position between Philemon and Onesimus, in Paul's mind the fact that they were brothers in Christ took precedence over their differences.

How should similar principles be seen today? *When someone does us wrong and they accept the Lord—we are to recieve them as a brother or sister in the Lord.*

C. PAUL'S REQUEST OF PHILEMON (*Phile. 17-21*). Any parent knows that the buildup to a request may be far longer than the request itself. In this case, Paul spent some time preparing Philemon for what he wanted Philemon to do. And so the request, when Paul finally stated it, likely came as no surprise.

*Examining the Text*

1. Read Philemon 17-21. What did Paul ask Philemon to do? (v. 17) *To recieve him as you would recieve me.*

How do you think Philemon felt when he finally read the request?

*Explaining the Text*

1. Since Paul had sent Onesimus to Philemon, it was logical that Paul would expect Onesimus to receive the same welcome that he himself would have received.

*Explaining the Text*

*Examining the Text*

2. What did Paul feel sure that Philemon would do? (v. 21) *Do even more than I say.*

3. Apparently part of Onesimus' offense included something that caused financial loss to his master Philemon. This could be simply the fact that Philemon lost his slave's services, or Onesimus may have taken money or goods from his master.

3. What did Paul promise to do in return? (v. 18)

*He would pay for anything (put on my account.)*

Would this have been an easy promise for Paul to fulfill? Why?

4. It is interesting that under his existing circumstances as a prisoner, the only way Paul could have repaid the debt to Philemon is through the gift from another. Ironically, perhaps it would even have been a gift from Philemon himself.

4. How did Paul address the matter of financial loss to Philemon and any outstanding debt? (v. 19)

*That I will repay*

How does this show wisdom and keen perception on Paul's part? *It shows how Paul like Christ wanted Onesimus debt settled - this illustration of our sins being imputed to Christ whereas God receives us in the merit of His Son.*

5. How would Philemon's positive response to Paul's request have encouraged Paul? (v. 20)

*To have joy from him in the Lord*

6. While some might feel that Paul was being presumptuous, his request may actually have been a reflection of the fact that Paul understood Philemon's

6. What more do you think that Paul would have liked for Philemon to do? (v. 21)

*That he would probably do whatever Paul requested due to the fact that Philemon*

| *Examining the Text* | *Explaining the Text* |
|---|---|
| Why do you think that Paul didn't specifically ask Philemon to do more? | character well. Paul also may have been keenly aware of a dramatic change in Onesimus' attitude and work. |

D. CLOSING AND BENEDICTION (*Phile. 22-25*). Just as we might do in concluding a letter today, Paul covered several miscellaneous items in his closing. He made one final request, and then shared greetings from the brothers at Rome.

| *Examining the Text* | *Explaining the Text* |
|---|---|
| 1. Read Philemon 22-25. How would Paul's being able to visit Philemon have been an answer to Philemon's prayers? (v. 22) *Through your prayers* | 1. Paul was hoping to visit Philemon, but we don't know for sure whether he ever actually had the opportunity. |
| 2. How do you think the key persons mentioned in this letter felt when it was read after Paul's execution? | |
| 3. What distinction did Paul make between Epaphras and the others who sent greetings? (v. 24) *Epaphras - fellow prisoner* *Others - fellow laborers.* | 3. Perhaps Epaphras was not actually a prisoner of Rome, but a brother who had chosen to place himself at Paul's service as a "prisoner" of Christ. |
| 4. How would the final closing have been particularly meaningful to both Onesimus and Philemon? (v. 25) | |

*Experiencing the Text*

1. If Paul were writing this letter to you today, what examples of your faithfulness in ministry might he cite as reason to express congratulations?

2. In what ways does Christianity remove barriers between individuals?


    What attitudes or relationships have been changed in your life because you are a follower of Christ?


3. What does this tiny book, with its heartfelt message, teach us about the quality of relationships within the body of Christ?


    How might these supersede or extend beyond mere legal requirements?